1971

Merry Christmas
and a Happy New Year.

Love,
Barbara, Lester
Nadine and Janet

The San Francisco I Love

the SAN

FRANCISCO I love...

Introduction by
JOSEPH L. ALIOTO
Mayor of the City of San Francisco

Photography by
PETER FINK

Text and captions by
JOYCE PETERSON

Edited and directed by
LÉON AMIEL

TUDOR PUBLISHING COMPANY
New York

Joseph L. ALIOTO.
Mayor

IT may be folly to introduce a lovely book on San Francisco by mentioning Los Angeles or, indeed, any of the spirited cities of California—San Diego and her graceful harbor; Sacramento and the State Capitol; Fresno and her vast farms; San Jose and her industry; and Eureka, Stockton, Santa Barbara, San Bernardino, and on through the State's glittering gazetteer. All share in the amazing growth of California, whose wealth and productivity rival all but the largest nations in the world.

The cities are united in the destiny of California, but San Francisco and Los Angeles share a special relationship. They are the centers which supply the essential energy of California's growth. They disburse the finances and provide the imagination that speed economic enterprise, cultural enhancement and human understanding. San Francisco and Los Angeles fuel California's unabated spirit of the forty-niners—the adventuresome pioneers who drove their covered wagons through the imposing Sierras, discovered gold, seeded the world's most prosperous agriculture and built the nation's most progressive industry.

That pioneering zeal now seeks the stars and new horizons to man's knowledge. Huge rockets are engineered for the moon and beyond and radio signals probe outermost space. California pulses with activity and with enormous aspiration that she can conquer not only the heavens but can create within her own boundaries an environment in which all men find justice and fulfillment.

San Francisco and Los Angeles share this sense of new frontiers, yet they differ in so many ways, and their differences give dimension to the phenomenal potential of all California.

It has become a kind of comic tradition for the two cities to snipe at one another—San Francisco spoofing Los Angeles' vast sprawl; Los Angeles needling San Francisco's impregnable chauvinism. There is no question that San Francisco has conspicuous pride in her traditions and in her continued glory. To some, this might seem conceit. It isn't.

San Francisco is a city with a soul, and her residents, whether they've lived 70 years in the City—(all California knows San Francisco as "The City")—or arrived on yesterday's jet, respond with true affection.

San Francisco has intense self-confidence, a collective spirit that insists on a sedulous pursuit of excellence. Given the option between two courses—one a safe, old method which perpetuates something that is just "good enough," the other, a new approach that gives the prudent prospect of greatness—I think it clear that the spirit of the times and the spirit of San Francisco tradition holds to the course of excellence.

She has always been a daring city. She brought her drinking water from the steep Sierras; she transformed dusty sand dunes into glorious Golden Gate Park; she spanned the churning waters of the Golden Gate with the majesty of a great bridge; and she tunneled the Bay for rapid transit.

San Francisco continues to build, enhancing her skyline but never sacrificing her distinctive architectural heritage. Vast towers pierce the sky; yet the city preserves the wondrous Victorian gingerbread of her turn-of-the-century elegance. Old waterfront warehouses are transformed into dazzling attractions—Ghirardelli Square and the Cannery. Urban renewal adds homes and industry, and the city wars against freeways that blot neighborhoods with concrete. San Francisco lives not in fear of an earthquake fault, but to the realization of an elementary goal—to give to every San Franciscan an equal opportunity to achieve the best of the human experience, in accordance with his or her capacity, in an urban environment that is at once peaceful, harmonious, beautiful and healthful.

San Francisco was founded just about the time the colonies on the continent's eastern seaboard began their restless march to rebellion. The splendid Mission Dolores was founded by the robed Franciscan fathers in 1776, the year of the shot heard around the world from the Concord green in Massachusetts.

By 1848, California was part of the United States, and that same year she made economically real the independence won the century before. Gold was discovered in the sparkling waters of the American River and made possible national emancipation from the monetary servitude to the wealthy nations of Europe.

The Gold Rush spirit of adventure and enterprise still characterizes San Francisco.

A reactionary retreat into nostalgia is a corruption of the California spirit, for change is a perennial fact of life and need not be feared. The Greek philosopher Heraclitus taught us that the only permanent thing in life is change. The human condition prospers best actually when there is a continuous interplay of the forces of innovation on the force of tradition.

For San Francisco to be San Francisco and to remain San Francisco, the arts and culture must continue to flourish, she must remain a mecca for the artist, the creative man, and the man with new ideas.

This city was enriched and its vitality was renewed by a constant flow of Europeans, Asiatics, South and Central Americans and our neighbors to the south, who left a life of despair and deprivation behind them in the hopes of a fresh beginning here. Just as my own father came here as an immigrant from a fisherman's family to build a business of his own, so too the hopes of a new beginning must be accorded to those who suffer deprivation in our own midst, and they in turn will enrich the City with their clearly predictable contributions to the common good.

I confess—if confession it be—to an unblushing affection for San Francisco. I like everything about her. Her jewelled panorama, her storied hills, her different peoples, her sparkling bay, her brisk fresh climate, her photogenic good looks—I even like her fog. San Francisco is a magnificent kaleidoscope of activities and neighborhoods and impressions. Tourists crowd Fisherman's Wharf. Chinatown adheres to ancient customs behind the veneer of souvenir shops. Hunters Point sheds her ghetto in a $ 50 million redevelopment planned by residents themselves. Cable cars clatter, and the Japanese Cultural Center blossoms with flowered kimonos.

So many impulses surge through her veins. She rocks with new music and poetry, and hums with the stately rhythms of opera, symphony and ballet companies that are among the most distinguished in the world. She builds mini-parks to add green to all her neighborhoods; and she plans huge commuter ships to convert San Francisco Bay into a magnificent thoroughfare. And always, she is at work building bridges between races to insure harmony and peace.

Many have attempted to capture the unique charm and flavor of San Francisco. Like all great charmers, she is all things to all men—a creature of many moods and faces. To the Italians she is Rome, Venice, Naples, Palermo and Florence, all rolled into one. To the sixty thousand Chinese who live here—Hong Kong in a western setting. To the English—the last civilized outpost. To the Irish—a spiritual frontier. To the Japanese, the best of East and West—the only city in the western world with a Kabuki theater. And to the native San Franciscan—the only place to live. Peter Fink has looked behind San Francisco's many faces and has brought her elusive essence into focus. Through his superb artistry, we take a new, penetrating look at our city, and savor anew the tempo and tastes, sights and sounds that are San Francisco's alone. For over a year, Peter Fink explored our city, turning his perceptive camera on the people and places that make San Francisco the most captivating and continental of all American cities. Wherever he went in this city of hills—from the alleys and bars of the Mission district to the drawing rooms and salons of Pacific Heights and Nob Hill—he recorded a warmly human documentary that is at once powerful and delicate, profound and poignant.

Peter Fink brings to this pictorial exploration of San Francisco the same master touch that made his tribute to his adopted city (The New York I Love) a classic.

Mr. Fink provides a living portrait of the character and the charm—and the challenge—of San Francisco. He brings into focus the dynamism and the leadership that make San Francisco distinctive and yet unite her with Los Angeles and all California in a fiery spirit of adventure that soars beyond the ordinary, beyond the complacent, beyond the mediocre, into the heights of the excellent, the daring and the imaginative.

Joseph L. ALIOTO.
Mayor

Joyce PETERSON

(Overleaf)

The eight and a half mile long San Francisco-Oakland Bay Bridge that connects the city with the east shore of the bay is the longest steel bridge in the world, and some thirty-five million vehicles a year cross it. This view is from the silent and mysterious shore of Yerba Buena Island, in the middle of San Francisco Bay. Civilians are not allowed on the island, as it is the property of the United States Navy, but thousands of motorists nevertheless rush through it day and night.

TWO hundred years ago the small, hilly peninsula that is now the city of San Francisco was covered with madrone and shifting sands. One hundred years ago it was a wild little seaport where adventurers from all over the world were drawn by the promise of quick money. Sixty years ago the same sandy peninsula was a smoldering ruin, ravaged and destroyed by earthquake and fire. Some said it was the hand of God, punishing the frivolous, high-living city. Others laughed and rebuilt it.

Today San Francisco is a shining, breathtaking and very self-conscious beauty of a city, sitting grandly on its splendid hills, swept clean by fog and wind, torn by love of its brief but heady past and the steady inroads of the twentieth century.

This hilly peninsula, caught between bay and sea, has had a flagrantly colorful history, from the Spanish caballeros who hunted and baited bears for sport, and the shaggy, gold-hunting forty-niners, to our own time when both the Beatniks, who discovered their identity in North Beach, and the Hippies, who cavorted in the Panhandle, are fading, too, into the history of the tolerant city. Such exotica will bloom again in San Francisco—the atmosphere is right for it—an atmosphere of easygoing permissiveness that has always respected a person's right to be different.

Robert O'Brien in *This is San Francisco* puts it this way:

13

"There were no cultural heritages in San Francisco, no Back Bay traditions, no snobbery, no phony class distinctions. Socially it was a free-for-all, and sooner or later society was bound to develop along lines established by the amount of cash with which you emerged from the scramble. This is a live and a let live town. Just by yourself, have a good time, and all the laughs you can get, and don't hurt anybody. That's all it asks...".

What else can you expect in a city where, in its early days, a man down on his luck could pick up fifty dollars a day by sifting floor sweepings for gold dust. The city had, and still has a raw style of its own—joyous, enthusiastic, wild.

You can see it in San Franciscans as they stride up and down their steep hills, as they jump onto the outside of a cable car, in bars, in restaurants. They smile a lot—they laugh a lot. They're good-time people—they always were.

San Francisco is the child of the forty-niners and will be until she gasps her last breath. As Rome lives with the legacy of the Caesars and Boston the Pilgrim Fathers, San Francisco lives with the memory of the brawling, brave, greedy, openhanded fortune hunters who risked their lives for gold and adventure.

Some of them died Croesus-rich in their huge, ghastly wooden palaces on Nob Hill; most of them died broke— cheerful, wiry old men who sat in the lobbies of cheap hotels and told people, again and again, what it had been like.

Fashionable apartments now scale the slopes of Telegraph Hill, to take advantage of the splendid views of the city, the Embarcadero and bay. Not long ago the hill was an art colony, goats roamed the grassy slopes and the city's bohemian population gathered to drink wine, to paint and to admire the same incomparable view.

The 4,200-foot span of the Golden Gate Bridge remained the world's largest from 1937, when it was built, until 1964, when the Verrazano Bridge in New York topped it. Twenty-five painters work full time to slosh two tons of "international orange" on it each week to keep it "golden."

And she is the child of the great railroad barons who tied the west to the east with a slim iron rail; and of the kings of the Comstock Lode who started out as saloon keepers; and of the hard-working whores and sleek gamblers and Sicilian fishermen and thousands of pig-tailed Chinese who built the railroad and did all the hard work for decades and brought the sounds and smells and colors of the Orient to the city.

All part of the city forever.

San Francisco was born rich. "Gold at Sutter's Mill" was the news that was to create the city and set its character for all times.

The city now lives on commerce, banking, shipping and the industrial titans of the west who run their empires from offices on Montgomery Street, but it was built on gold—an endless stream of little leather bags of grey-brown gold dust. Gold was to make San Francisco a legendary city, a magnet for the young, the footloose, the adventurous, anyone who was willing to risk his life and endure great discomforts for the chance to make his fortune.

The untapped wealth of the west was spilling into men's hands and San Francisco was "The City" where they banked it and spent it. (Always "The City," and her citizens always dressed to the nines. No "town" this, even when "streets" were muddy rivers and sidewalks nonexistent.)

San Francisco was market place, pleasure palace, the entrance and the exit, the hub of the west. The huge bay was the gateway to and the exit from the west and

Telegraph Hill still bears the scars inflicted on it by the Grey brothers, who blasted away at their convenient stone quarry until, in 1910, a twelve—room house toppled over the brink and smashed to bits on Sansome Street below. The local residents protested with considerable violence and stopped the blasting before the hill was chipped away completely.

(Overleaf)

A telephoto lens draws the wooded hills of Oakland and Berkeley close to downtown San Francisco. ·Actually they are more than ten miles away. Market Street, the large thoroughfare in the center, bisects the city.

21

the city became port, banker and shopkeeper to the entire territory. More riches poured into the city when the Comstock Lode, a fantastic vein of pure silver, was discovered in Nevada. And in rapid succession all the profits of a rich virgin territory found its way to San Francisco.

This was easy money, not painfully scratched from a reluctant New England soil, but ready money that gave itself up easily to those who looked. The climate was as amiable as the land—no numbing winter, no scorching summer to be endured.

You may imagine that the virtues of thrift and conservatism would have difficulty catching hold in such a town. The newness of the land was a great social leveller. Pomposity was impossible, "background" meant nothing here where a man could if he chose assume a new identity as easily as he might slip on a new coat. Achievement was everything, and humor and tolerance, to replace the bigotry and small-mindedness that many had come west to flee.

The young city and its energetic citizens grabbed at wealth and speedily ordered life's material joys shipped out from Europe and the east. Fine wines, theater, music, expensive furniture, and clothes, the more elaborate the better—all paid for by the endless little bags of gold panned by dirty, bearded miners who lived for months at a time in barbarously uncomfortable camps, patiently panning and panning, sifting and sifting, putting the precious stuff into little bags and finally arriving, filthy, triumphant and rich in the brawling city that

Tucked away under the sedate palms of Union Square, a four-level garage hums with activity. The underground garage, built in 1942, was the first such structure in the world. The buildings which surround Union Square were put up just after the 1906 earthquake, and many of the city's finest shops have been there ever since.

offered all the coarser joys of civilization for a price, and a high one.

Most of the miners, after a splendid week of gambling, drinking, whoring and fighting headed, dead broke, back to the camps, lucky to save a new shirt and mining pan out of the bacchanal.

The more unfortunate were drugged and shanghaied in seedy Barbary Coast bars, and found themselves sobering up with a dreadful headache, bound for a three—year cruise to China or Alaska.

These are the people and these are the circumstances that made the city. Extraordinary people drawn by extraordinary circumstances. The easygoing atmosphere soon affected even the most sobersided Easterners who trekked west. Richard Henry Dana, in 1849, describes the transformation of a recent arrival.

"Indeed, I found individuals as well as public bodies affected in a marked degree by a change of oceans and California life. One Sunday afternoon I was surprised at receiving the card of a man whom I had last known as a strict and formal deacon of a Congregational society in New England. He was a deacon still, in San Francisco, a leader in all pious works, devoted to his denomination and to total abstinence—the same internally, but externally what a change! Gone was the downcast eye, the bated breath, the solemn non-natural voice, the watchful gait, stepping as if he felt responsible for the balance of the moral universe. He walked with a stride, and uplifted open countenance, his face covered with beard, whiskers and moustache, his voice strong

Since 1938, the thirty-three eucalyptus and pine covered acres of Sigmund Stern Grove have been the scene of outdoor concerts, opera, light opera and theatricals. Arthur Fiedler conducts Pops concerts here each summer, and as many as 20,000 people have gathered around the amphitheatre, some on the wooden benches, more on the ground on the hillside under the trees, to listen. All performances are free.

26

The three Pacific Heights houses in the photograph below were built, respectively, in the late 1860's or 70's, and in 1895. Today they are painted in dramatic complementary colors. The Casebolt House, right, also in Pacific Heights, was built in opulent Italianate style in 1866 for Henry Casebolt, a blacksmith from Virginia who emigrated to San Francisco with his wife and eleven children.

and natural—in short he had put off the New England deacon and become a human being."

They almost didn't find it. Ships of six nations sailed up and down the rocky and inhospitable coast of California for two hundred years before the great silent bay hidden by the sandy, scrub-covered peninsula was discovered.

Sir Francis Drake roamed the coast on the Golden Hinde in 1579, and incidentally nailed a brass plate to a post to declare that the coast was part of "The Kingdom of Her Majesty Queen Elizabeth and Her Successors forever," but though he and his crew paused to shoot seals on the Farallon Islands just twenty-six miles offshore from the Golden Gate, they neglected to find the entrance to the bay, which remained sleeping silently behind its curtain of fog two centuries longer.

The bay was still undiscovered when three hundred miles to the south the Mexican village of Los Angeles teemed with activity, burros and stray dogs, and fifty miles north, near the cathedral stillness of the redwood forests the Russians had established a fur station called Fort Ross.

Mariners searched almost in vain for a safe berth on the difficult coast, and still the great bay remained invisible. The sand dunes that were to be San Francisco were the hunting and fishing preserve of a primitive band of roving Indians who preferred, for habitation, the warmer eastern shore.

Then in 1769 an expedition led overland by Gaspar de Portola came upon the bay. Portola saw it only as

The Mechanics' Monument, upper left, is a memorial to Peter Donahue, who built the first foundry in San Francisco. Fauns and turtles, lower left, play around the base of a copy of a sixteenth-century fountain in Nob Hill's Huntington Park. The park was given to the city by the widow of Collis B. Huntington, one of the "big four" railroad magnates, after the Huntington mansion on the site burned down in 1906. Marcello Mascherini's "Running Lady," left, dramatizes the foyer of the Crown-Zellerbach Building, headquarters of one of the nation's biggest pulp and paper companies. Crown-Zellerbach's head, J.D. Zellerbach, a leader in efforts to enhance the beauty of the city, gave nearly two-thirds of the building site to enlarge nearby Mechanics' Square.

Since the first Sicilian fisherman sailed into the bay some hundred and twenty years ago and hauled back nets loaded with crab, San Franciscans have been magnetized by the lure of Fisherman's Wharf. In the old days, fishermen sold the day's catch directly from their boats.

The huge restaurants overlooking Fisherman's Wharf are usually thronged with San Franciscans and tourists alike. The tradition of the Wharf is so completely Italian that when two enterprising restaurateurs named McAteer and Sweeny decided to open a restaurant here, they named it Tarantino's.

an obstacle to further exploration, and returned to Monterey. Not until six years later did a little Spanish packet, the San Carlos, set off to find the entrance to the bay Portola had seen.

The first Spanish settlers arrived a year later. The few soldiers and their families called the peninsula Yerba Buena (good herb) after a mintlike herb they found growing in abundance, built a few houses and settled down to an idyllic life. Dedicated horsemen and hunters, little interested in farming or boating on the bay, they raised horses, baited bears, pitting them against fighting bulls for sport, and left the land virtually untouched. They were unconcerned with the outside world, and as removed from it as they might have been on another planet.

Their idyllic life came to a sudden end in 1846 when the Yankee ship *Portsmouth* sailed into the harbor and declared the town the possession of the United States. Commander John Montgomery of the United States Navy hoisted the Stars and Stripes in the plaza (now Portsmouth Square) and the simple carefree life of the Spanish settlers was at an end. Their lands were confiscated and they were overwhelmed by the energetic Yankees who came pouring out from the east.

An ambitious alcalde, Washington Bartlett, changed the name of the settlement from Yerba Buena to San Francisco. (He reasoned that taking the name of the bay would stimulate the growth of the small community, which was then engaged in considerable rivalry with Benicia, a settlement on the north end of the bay.)

The new 52-story corporate headquarters of the Bank of America looms over two older buildings in the financial district. Dominating the plaza, named after A.P. Giannini, in front of the building is a gigantic (13 by 25 foot) oval sculpture of smooth black Swedish granite by sculptor Masayiki Nagare, which has already been dubbed by San Franciscans—"The Banker's Heart."
The building in the right foreground, though apparently designed for the ages, has been razed, and is now just one more vanished San Francisco landmark.

Then in 1848 news arrived, in the form of a quinine bottle, which was to change the face of San Francisco and California—indeed, of the entire west—in a matter of months. The news was gold.

James Marshall discovered gold by accident in a creek at Sutter's Mill, a small sawmill on a huge tract of land in the foothills of the Sierras. John Sutter, who owned the land, dreamed of turning it into a vast and prosperous ranch. Sensing disaster for his plans, Sutter tried to keep the discovery secret, but soon the rumors had travelled to the coast.

The stories were confirmed when Sam Brannan, who kept a small shop on the American River, went to look for himself, filled a quinine bottle with the precious dust and brought it to San Francisco. Waving the bottle in the streets, he cried "gold, gold at Sutter's Mill," and the rush was on. Every ambulatory male in San Francisco dropped what he was doing and headed for the gold fields.

John Sutter's alarm was well founded. His ranch was overrun by miners who occupied his land at will. He finally retired to a small holding high in the Sierras. James Marshall died without a penny to his name.

In 1847 the population of San Francisco was four hundred and fifty. By the end of 1848 twenty-five thousand men had jammed into the town. Ships were abandoned and sunk in the bay as their crews departed *en masse* for the gold fields. An egg cost a dollar, laundry was shipped to the Hawaiian Islands or China for want of anyone to scrub a shirt locally. Crime was rampant;

This imposing structure at 3640 Buchanan Street was originally the San Francisco Gas Light Building, built in 1893. The main room once housed two great gas compression cylinders. Over the years the building has passed through several hands, and is currently a fashionable antique and flower shop called Merryvale.

MDCCCXXXVII
TO
· RAPHAEL · WEILL ·
OFFICIER · DE · LA · LEGION · D'HONNEVR ·
NATIVE · OF · FRANCE ·

Outside the California Palace of the Legion of Honor "The Shades" by Rodin stands stark against blue sky and wind-swept trees. A relaxed summer crowd ambles through an art exhibit casually assembled on the grass at Washington Square in North Beach. Portsmouth Square, right, was San Francisco's first civic center, where citizens traded, debated and loafed. The American flag was first raised here in 1846, and it was here that discovery of gold was announced in 1848.

there were more than four thousand murders committed in the mid-1850's.

Bayard Taylor in *El Dorado* describes the city by night.

"The appearance of San Francisco, by night, from the water, is unlike anything I ever beheld. The houses are mostly of canvas, which is made transparent by the lamps within, and transforms them, in the darkness, to dwellings of solid light. Seated on the slopes of its three hills, the tents pitched among the chapparal to the very summits, it gleams like an amphitheatre of fire. Here and there shine out brilliant points, from the decoy lamps of the gaming houses, and through the indistinct murmur of the streets comes by fits the sound of music from their hot and crowded precincts. The picture has in it something unreal and fantastic; it impresses one like the cities of the magic lantern, which a motion of the hand can build or anihilate."

From the time Bayard Taylor described the tent city of 1849, the town grew at a spectacular rate. The settlement burned to the ground six times between 1849 and 1854, and was rebuilt with both good cheer and remarkable speed each time.

Though its citizens loved it, and most visitors were fascinated by the city in its raw, booming days, there were dissenters. Anthony Trollope, writing in 1875 grumbled:

"I do not know that in all my travels I ever visited a city less interesting to the normal tourist than San Francisco. There is a new park in which you may drive

The huge dome of Temple Emanu-El looms magnificently above the surrounding houses on Arguallo Boulevard. The building, a modern interpretation of Byzantine, was completed in 1926.

Andrew Hillidie's cable car made its first successful trial run in 1873, to everyone's astonishment, and to many people's continuing astonishment the cable cars are running still, a tribute to the triumph of common sense over financial statistics. From their heyday when there were twelve cable car lines running in San Francisco, they have dwindled to three. At left, the Powell Street car begins its ascent of Nob Hill, and above, the California Street car climbs Nob Hill, and reaches the end of its rope in Polk Gulch.

for six or seven miles on a well made road. The park will, when completed, have many excellencies. There is the biggest hotel in the world, just finished but not yet opened when I was there. There is an inferior menagerie of wild beasts, and a place called The Cliff House, to which strangers are taken to hear seals bark...."

Despite the disapprobation of Anthony Trollope, the city grew and prospered wildly. Paving replaced the rough lumber that had covered the streets, impressive buildings sprang up almost overnight, the Palace, the largest, some say the grandest hotel the world had ever seen was built on Market Street (destined to flourish and glitter for thirty years, and burn to the ground in the fire of 1906). The baroque Nob Hill palaces appeared, and San Francisco's lovely park continued to emerge, like a green Eden, from the barren dunes.

San Franciscans, then as now, were in the habit of thinking big. They wanted the best of everything for their new town, and decided a park was needed. Fortunately, at the right moment they were inspired by the right man, Frederick Law Olmsted, who had designed Central Park in New York. Olmsted recommended to San Franciscans that they build "a pleasure ground second to none in the world, for the convenience not merely of the present population or even of their immediate successors, but of many millions of people." It sounded like a good idea.

Millionaire Sam Brannan (the same Sam Brannan who waved the quinine bottle full of dust and started the

The city and the San Francisco-Oakland Bay Bridge are a misty shadow in the distance from the flower-bedecked terrace of a house in Belvedere.

gold rush) and many other citizens with both power and money agreed.

A committee formed to select a site for the park considered the Presidio, with its magnificent view of the Golden Gate. They considered the Mission district, as the land was protected in the lee of Twin Peaks. And finally decided upon a vast, empty tract that had nothing to recommend it but its size (huge) and price (small).

They purchased a half-mile wide strip of land that stretched from the geographical center of San Francisco to the ocean. All of it was sand dune, and sensible folk suggested that nothing could possibly be persuaded to grow there. However, the few squatters who lived on the bleak expanse were forcibly expelled and the task of converting the wasteland into a park was begun.

The monumental work of turning the dunes into "a park second to none" fell into the hands of a young engineer, William Hammond Hall, chosen because he was familiar with the area, having mapped it for the United States Army. Hall was young, enthusiastic, and, best of all, believed, when few others did, that the dunes *could* become a park.

He began his search for something to hold the shifting sands; tried the native lupine, but without much success. He then learned that in Europe loose brush was scattered over soil to protect new seedlings, but in the sand hills of San Francisco there was not enough brush available to cover the endless dunes. The solution came by accident, when his horse knocked

The City Hall, top, was built in 1913 by architects Bakewell and Brown. The Classical Baroque building with its heroic proportions, giant dome and finely finished detailing is a perfect example of the era's concept of what a civic building should be. The grand design of San Francisco's civic center still makes it the most splendid in the United States. The War Memorial Building is to the left of the elaborate iron gates, the Opera House to the right. The gates themselves are the carriage entrance to the Opera House.
Bonanza king James C. Flood's mansion, below, was the only one of the many grand houses on Nob Hill to survive the 1906 fire. The Italianate-Baroque palace, built in 1885 at an estimated cost of $1,500,000 is now the home of the Pacific Union Club (known to San Franciscans, affectionately, as the P. U. Club).

The Powell Street cable car is still turned by
hand at the Market Street turntable by the joint
efforts of the conductor and the gripman, and the
huge wheels still whir steadily to pull the giant
cable that shuttles the cars up and down the hills.
Firemen, above, race down California Street.

over a bucket of barley on which he had been feeding. Hall scooped up the sandy feld, but his horse refused it. Hall threw away the barley, a light rain fell, and the barley sprouted in the sand. Here was a cover to hold the sand well enough to begin!

Hardy young trees followed; Monterey pine and cyprus, eucalyptus and acacia. In an almost miraculous six years the park began to turn green and became a prime attraction in the city.

When Hall retired, he picked as his successor a dedicated young Scot named John McLaren, who was to remain, for the next fifty years, the builder, protector, and guiding genius of the park.

McLaren had the notion that parks were for people. He refused to put up "keep off the grass" signs, battled those who wanted to formalize the park in the manner of Versailles, and fought developers who persistently attempted to nibble away at bits and pieces of the land. When city officials granted promoters permission to run a trolley line through the park, "provided it would not disturb existing trees or flowers," McLaren hastened to the barricades with an army of gardeners, planted groves of trees and flower beds almost overnight in the path of the offending trolley line. The promoters withdrew.

He particularly loathed the statues which were constantly being donated to the park, and promptly planted shrubbery around them to shield them from public view.

Today, if you should visit the Rhododendron Dell

The San Francisco hills are rapidly being levelled by new office buildings which dwarf them. Some of the recent additions are, left to right; the grey granite and ceramic Standard Oil Building on Market Street, whose twenty-two stories went up in 1965; the aluminum and glass tower of the Wells-Fargo, also 1965, and forty-three stories; and the Crown-Zellerbach Building, considered a giant in 1959. The glass, aluminum and Italian mosaic tile Crown-Zellerbach is gracefully placed in more than an acre of city-enhancing walkways and gardens.

that was his special pride and joy, you will find a statue of John McLaren (he would have hated it) with a pine cone in his hand. But ever respectful of their beloved Uncle John, the gardeners placed the statue, not on a pedestal, but on the grass he loved so well.

★

In 1873 Andrew Hallidie solved the problem of transportation on San Francisco's steep hills by inventing the cable car.

By 1889 there were eight cable car lines sliding silently about the city, and Rudyard Kipling described them:

"The cable cars have for all practical purposes made San Francisco a dead level. They take no count of rise or fall, but slide equably on their appointed courses from one end to the other of a six-mile street. They turn corners at right angles; cross other lines, and, for aught I know may run up the sides of houses. There is no visible agency of their flight; but once in a while you shall pass a five-storied building, humming with machinery that winds up an everlasting wire-cable, and the initiated will tell you that here is the mechanism. I gave up asking questions. If it pleases Providence to make a car run up and down a slit in the ground for many miles, and for two-pence halfpenny I can ride in that car, why shall I seek the reasons of the miracle?"

By the turn of the century San Francisco was a booming, laughing, dashing town, proud of its park, cable cars, opera, symphonies, opulence and women.

The Conservatory in Golden Gate Park has been a San Francisco landmark since 1876, when it was shipped round the Horn from New York in thousands of small pieces. The Conservatory was a gift from pioneer James Lick, who just the year before had sold for $175,000 a downtown lot he had purchased in the 1850's for $300.

Kipling again, said: "San Francisco is a mad city—inhabited for the most part by perfectly insane people whose women are of a remarkable beauty."

And then on April 18, 1906, disaster struck. The city was almost completely destroyed by earthquake and a fire that raged uncontrollably for days. From that time San Francisco history was reckoned by "before the fire" and "after the fire."

When the news of the destruction of the city reached New York, the exiled San Franciscan Will Irwin wrote:

"The old San Francisco is dead. The gayest, lightest-hearted, most pleasure-loving city of the western continent, and in many ways the most interesting and romantic, is a horde of refugees living among the ruins. It may rebuild; it probably will; but those who have known that particular city by the Golden Gate, have caught its particular flavor of the Arabian Nights, feel that it can never be the same. It is as though a pretty, frivolous woman had passed through a great tragedy. She survives, but she is sobered and different. If it rises out of the ashes it must be a modern city, much like other cities and without its old atmosphere."

Will Irwin was not entirely right. The spirit of San Francisco was not to be crushed by any fire or earthquake. True, the Barbary Coast never again achieved its pre-fire heights of venality, and the bars where sailors were shanghaied flourished no more, but the best of the city was soon rebuilt in the florid style of the area, and San Franciscans were soon pursuing their same rounds of business and pleasure, and still

Grant Avenue at night is aglow with the cultural cross-pollination of neon, ancient Chinese lettering, and the ghostly patterns that automobile headlights trace on a time exposure.

56

Chinatown changes but survives. Tourists flock here by the thousands, to pace along Grant Avenue, to buy souvenirs in the small shops, few of which have had any genuine Chinese merchandise to offer for decades. But the area is still home to thousands of Chinese who eat their own food, read their own newspapers, play their own games.

A century ago the district was considered so sinful by the Paulist Fathers of St. Mary's, far right, that they inscribed "Son, observe the time and fly from evil" under the church clock. The admonition can be seen there still.

laughing with the same characteristic irreverence.

One of the few structures to survive the holocaust was the Hotaling Building, which was used as a distillery. This inspired poet Charles Field to enquire:

"If, as they said, God spanked the town,
For being over-frisky,
Why did he burn the churches down,
And spare Hotaling's Whiskey?"

San Francisco's humor, tolerance, and from time to time unabashed sentimentality is best exemplified by its affection for its very own eccentrics, who would be shunned if not actually put away in more serious-minded towns.

Scarcely a book exists on San Francisco that does not bear some loving reference to Iodoform Kate. Now Iodoform Kate was quite simply a leather-lunged madam who occupied lodgings on Morton Street, a small street occupied completely by houses of prostitution. (Morton Street, re-christened and reformed, is now the demure, shop-lined Maiden Lane.) Iodoform Kate exploited her hard-working girls and sniffed iodoform for diversion. San Franciscans found her amusing. And then there was "The Great Unknown" who spoke to no one, "Oofty-Goofty," a poor old madman who invited anyone to hit him for a dime, and the most beloved and appealing folk-hero of all, the Emperor Norton.

Joshua Norton was a gentle lunatic whose mind gave way from a business reverse in 1854. (A prosperous

The *Amazarashi-No-Hotoke Buddha —The Buddha That Sits Through Sunny and Rainy Weather—from the Toconji Temple in Japan now meditates amidst the rhododendrons in the Japanese Tea Garden in Golden Gate Park. Hostesses from the Japanese Tea Garden pause for a portrait.*

It would be hard to imagine San Francisco without the familiar, smiling faces of Chinese children—off to Chinese school, trudging down Telegraph Hill with their parents, smiling for a picture on Broadway.

merchant, he had tried to corner the rice market, and failed.) From then on he absented his mind from petty cares and assumed those of a more cosmic scale. Styling himself Norton I, Emperor of the United States and Protector of Mexico, *Gracias Dei,* he wore splendidly epauletted uniforms of his own design, issued bonds that were accepted by all San Francisco tradesmen, corresponded with Queen Victoria and Alexander of Russia, and once asked the widowed Queen's hand in marriage.

Apart from his conviction that he was Emperor of the United States and Protector of Mexico, Joshua Norton was a rational, charming and well-informed man who lived in a small furnished room (fifty cents a night, which sum he paid each evening) and spent much of his time in local libraries keeping up on current events which he discussed with his many friends on daily rounds of the city. It was his custom to visit favored acquaintances, chat for an hour or two, and go on his way. For years he was accompanied by two mongrel dogs, Bummer and Lazarus, and when the faithful Bummer died thousands of San Franciscans attended his funeral, as they later respectfully did for the gentle Emperor himself.

Still another eccentric heroine of the same era was Lily Hitchcock Coit, a respectable maiden of impeccable family and fortune, whose pleasure it was to gallop off to fires whenever she heard the alarm. She had herself photographed with a whiskey bottle in her hand in an era when whiskey and ladies were not mentioned in the same breath, and so proud was she of her honorary

A bank in Chinatown looks like a Tinker Toy version of a Chinese temple. The local Chinese are at odds in their opinion of such buildings. Some find them deplorable and call the style "pigtail architecture"; others, more concerned with finance than aesthetics frankly advocate putting on "a Hollywood facade to attract tourists."

membership in the San Francisco Volunteer Fire Department that she signed herself Lily Hitchcock Coit, 5, until she died at eighty-four.

We have Lily Coit and her enthusiasm for firemen to thank for Coit Tower. In her will she left a sum of money for a "suitable memorial" to be erected atop Telegraph Hill in honor of her beloved firemen.

The affection for eccentrics persists to this day. Among the contemporary folk heroes is Sally Stanford, a madam who became famous in the 1940's for her continuous battles with the San Francisco police. She was determined to pursue her vocation on Bush Street, the constabulary was determined she should not. Her name became a household word as newspapers reported her barbed witticisms in frequent verbal skirmishes. Miss Stanford eventually capitulated and retired to Sausalito, where she opened a highly successful restaurant.

Then there was the unforgettable Ding Dong Daddy of the D Line, an amorous street car conductor who won the hearts of his fellow citizens when the news came out that he had for some years coped successfully with some half-dozen wives. And we must not forget Tiny Armstrong, a chubby, good-natured, minor-league eccentric who made quite a name for himself by simply traipsing around town in funny costumes, and blowing a bird whistle.

Unsurprisingly, this is the town where, for better or worse, "topless" made its debut. (Nothing new, in fact. Customers in some of the wilder Barbary Coast boîtes were served by nude waitresses in the 1860's.) Locals

A Japanese bridge casts its curved reflection in a still pond of the Japanese Tea Garden in Golden Gate Park.

*S*an Francisco's War Memorial Opera House was built as a remembrance to those who served in the First World War. The city was the first in the nation to build a civic opera house, and the first to vote municipal support for a symphony orchestra. Opening night at the opera is a glittering event. The Opera House is brilliantly lit, opera-goers dress to the nines, and afterwards gather for the Post-Opera Supper next door in the auditorium of the Veteran's Memorial Building.

THE CHILDREN OF THE WORLD SHALL INHERIT THE EARTH

are yawning (or giggling) over "topless" already. A sign in Vesuvio, a witty little bar in North Beach, advises that they have "booths for topless lady psychiatrists." Meanwhile night club owners happily rake in money from boggle-eyed tourists.

This is the town where female impersonators have been a favorite attraction for years—nothing sordid, just good, bawdy San Francisco fun for the family. A city, to sum it up, where few hypocritical moral judgments are made, where the name of a sharp-tongued madam may be more familiar than that of a city councilman, and which, all in all, ambles along with no more (probably less) vice and crime than any other metropolis whose city fathers froth and fret in a vain attempt to impose their notions of respectability on a reluctant populace.

Writing for the Scottish Daily Mail, Bernard Levin, a recent visitor, comments with some astonishment on the tolerance that San Francisco takes for granted. He had observed the (Communist) Daily Worker for sale in a vending machine nestled undisturbed just outside the doorway of the (right wing) John Birch Society headquarters. But of course.

★

You don't know San Francisco until you know the fog. Fog is the Wagnerian element in the city—its mantle of dignity, its melancholy soul.

On a bright, clear day the city is possessed of an almost maddening exhilaration, when the air, with its

Beniamino Bufano's giant steel statue of a hand is inscribed: "The Children of the World Shall Inherit the Earth." A lifelong pacifist, Mr. Bufano cut off one his own fingers and sent it to Woodrow Wilson as a protest against the United States entry into the First World War.

San Francisco is a city surrounded by water. The tremendous engineering feat accomplished in spanning the bay becomes clear in this aerial photograph of the San Francisco-Oakland Bay Bridge. Watery reflections, right, are boats floating at anchor in Belvedere.

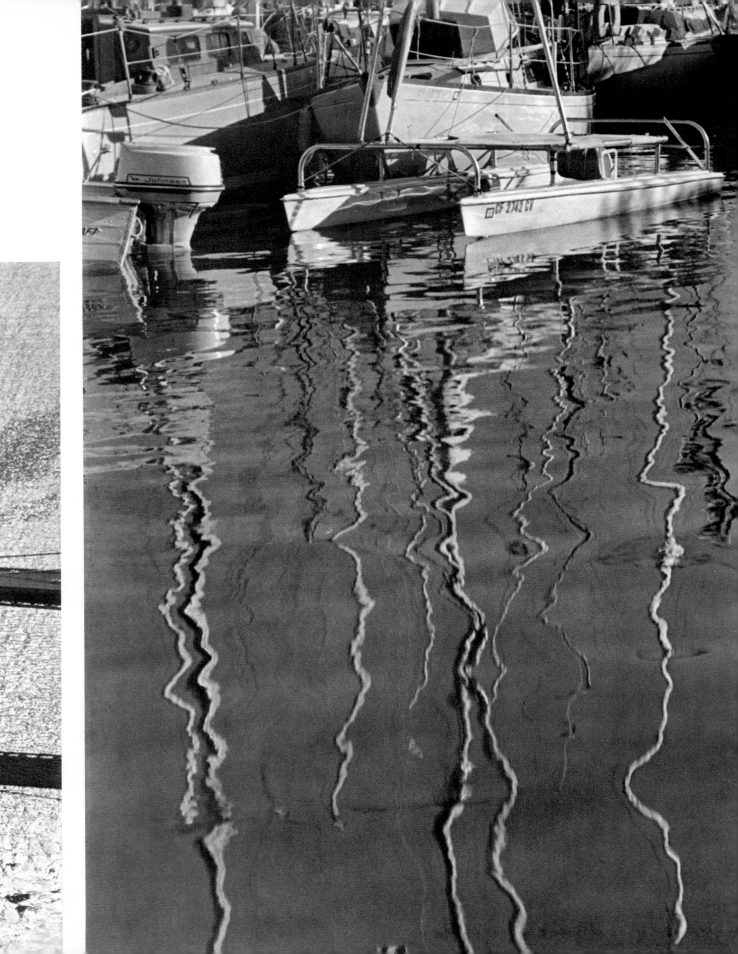

slight ocean chill, is clear as an ice-chip and smells of sea and ships and redwood trees, roasting coffee and spices, fish and acacia and geraniums grown wild. On days like this, when the wind-driven fog comes tearing in, the city can become drowned in melancholy. This is when San Franciscans hasten to the warm cheer, the conviviality of their bars and restaurants, fleeing the fog.

Just a few miles inland householders may be sitting in their sunny gardens, barbecuing chicken, open-shirted, domestic. This is not a San Francisco scene. The fog takes care of that—makes it an indoor town—a brisk, energetic, walking town.

Ninety years ago, when Robert Louis Stevenson visited California, he took refuge in a cabin high on the slopes of Mt. St. Helena, sixty miles to the north of the city, mostly to escape the summer fogs.

One day the fog crept into Napa Valley and found him even there in his eyrie. He left a haunting description of it:

"In their place [the foothills] not a thousand feet below me, rolled a great level ocean. It was as though I had gone to bed the night before safe in a nook of inland mountains, and had awakened in a bay on the coast. And when I was yet doubting, a promentory of the hills some four or five miles away, conspicuous by a bouquet of tall pines, was in a single instant overtaken and swallowed up. It reappeared in a little while with its pines, but this time on an islet, and only to be swallowed up once more and then for good. I could trace its

A reproduction of a Japanese pagoda in the Buddhist style of the Nara era attracts visitors to the Japanese Tea Garden. The best time to visit the Garden is in April, when the cherry trees and azaleas are in full bloom.

progress, one pine tree first growing hazy and disappearing after another; although sometimes there was none of this forerunning haze, but the whole opaque white ocean gave a start and swallowed a piece of mountain at a gulp.

"It was to flee these poisonous fogs that I had left the seaboard and climbed so high among the mountains. And now, behold, here came the fog to besiege me in my chosen altitudes, and yet came so beautifully that my first thought was of welcome."

Will Irwin's description of the climate of San Francisco in 1906 is accurate today:

"The climate of California is peculiar. In the region about San Francisco all the forces of nature work on their own laws. There is no thunder and lightning; there is no snow, except a flurry every five or six years; there are perhaps half-a-dozen nights in the winter when the thermometer drops low enough so that in the morning there is a little film of ice on exposed water. Neither is there any hot weather. Yet most Easterners remaining in San Francisco for a few days remember that they were always chilly.

"For the Gate is a big funnel, drawing in the winds and the mists which cool off the great, hot interior valleys of the San Joaquin and Sacramento. So the west wind blows steadily ten months of the year; and almost all the mornings are foggy.

"This keeps the temperature steady at about fifty-five

The Eastern Orthodox Cathedral of the Holy Virgin combines classical onion-shaped turrets with modern architecture. The six saints on the facade, presented in the frontal aspect in the tradition derived from Ravenna and Constantinople, seem quite at home on Geary Street.

The Palace of Fine Arts designed by Bernard Maybeck, below and lower left, was built of wood lathe and papier-mâché as a temporary fantasy for the Exposition of 1915, but San Franciscans loved the romantic structure so dearly that they could never bear to tear it down. Time and weather eventually threatened to do what they would not, until a recent grant from industrialist Walter Johnson sparked a rescue and restored the building to permanent grandeur.

The California Palace of the Legion of Honor, upper left, looking especially grand with night-time illumination, is an exact copy of the Palais de la Légion d'Honneur in Paris.

degrees—a little cool for the comfort of an unacclimated person, especially indoors.

"Californians, used to it, hardly ever think of making fires except in a few days of the winter season, and then they rely mainly upon fireplaces. This is like the custom of the Venetians and the Florentines."

The Embarcadero, San Francisco's romantically named waterfront, now a peaceful and decorative commercial adjunct to the city, was once its center, its heartbeat, its source of news, life, goods, and its only connection with the outside world.

The Embarcadero has seen strange and glorious days. Strange days when ships were abandoned and sat like creaking ghosts, their crews racing to the gold fields; glorious days when the clipper ships triumphantly arrived in full sail after their terrible voyages round the Horn. So eager was the isolated town for news of the ships that a semaphore atop Telegraph Hill flashed the news of every arrival, describing the ship, its contents, crew, and in the early days, one more vital statistic, the number of women on board.

From here the First California Battalion sailed, laughing and cheering, off to the Spanish-American War, some to return, some to die in the jungles of the Philippines.

And many a San Franciscan can clearly recall the foggy day in 1945 when half the town trudged to Russian Hill and the foot of Coit Tower to patiently watch a silent drama. With the hills as amphitheatre and the bay the stage, Admiral Halsey brought the Third Fleet back from the Pacific.

In the 1920's the first paved road was built to the top of Telegraph Hill, and soon after, Coit Tower was constructed as a memorial to San Francisco's firemen, with money left for that purpose by Lily Hitchcock Coit. Today San Franciscans have grown accustomed to the tower, but in the beginning it drew violent objections. Lady Honore Cecelia Bowlby-Gledhill attained immortality one night in the early 1930's by crying to her companions, "Boys, I don't like that silo," and then firing the contents of a pistol into it.

W*ater, water everywhere and plenty of ships, skiffs and sailboats to go fishing and sailing all year long. Sausalito, right, is still and silent, and just ten minutes from the city.*

Robert O'Brien describes it in *This is San Francisco.*

"Two blimps, grey like the sky, suddenly poked their blunt noses through the fog and hovered close to the water. A thin, dark submarine emerged from the mist and knifed slowly up the stream, inshore and close to the Embarcadero.

"It was ten minutes to one when the first whistles came from the ships at the North Beach piers. Soon the people on Telegraph Hill saw what the men on the ships down there had seen before them—the low hull of a destroyer escort. Inch by inch (so slowly did it seem to travel), it slid into view from behind the corner of an apartment house between the hill and the Bay.

"And, one by one, the destroyers moved up past the waterfront. The welcoming horns and whistles blew, and against their bass the yelp of a ship's siren rose and fell. There was a fireboat off Fisherman's Wharf, and suddenly water feathered from her nozzles in four white plumes. Like the grim ghosts of ships came the others— the cruiser *Vicksburg,* her blinker lights flashing shoreward; the battleship *South Dakota,* with her victory pennant trailing like a serpent across her stern.

"Dark and menacing, their guns angled slightly toward the sky, they stole silently up the Bay. Behind each of them followed a school of tiny, eager landing craft, and behind the landing craft were the white, spreading wakes.

"All at once there was that glad burst of the Ferry Building siren, sending its weird and triumphant anthem across the Bay. In the waterfront factories and ware-

Locally grown flowers are sold on the street the year round in the amiable San Francisco climate. Most come from the Flower Terminal, a giant wholesale market at Sixth and Brannan Streets, which comes as a delightful surprise in an otherwise uninspiring district.

houses, workmen tied the whistles down and let them blow.

"On the hill, the crowd began to break up, and there was the sound of many automobiles starting at one. The school children formed their lines and marched back to their school on Union Street, and hill dwellers, who had watched from their windows and roof tops, put away their field glasses and returned to the open fires you knew about because there was in the air, and had been all morning, the smell of smoke from the coal they use in their fireplaces up there on the hill.

"Soon the people had all gone, and the hill again belonged to the gloomy sky and the still, dripping trees.

"Down below the hill and around the base of the hill was the Embarcadero, black and slick in the fog. Ships coming home were an old story to that street. That's what it was there for, that was its life.

"It lay waiting for them."

San Francisco was on its way to being a cosmopolitan town when its city hall was a tent. In 1849 there were already several flourishing French restaurants, a good sized German one, a *Fonda Peruana,* The Italian Confectionery, and three Chinese restaurants that were extremely popular not only because the food was first rate (paradise indeed, for a miner back from the diggings) but for the fact that all meals cost exactly one dollar no matter what you ate.

The Argonauts (settlers who arrived before the Gold Rush) numbered among them many Europeans of consid-

The twenty-five story *Alcoa Building presents a sheer handsome wall of bronze and glass with an unusual diagonal cross-hatch design. Structural bracing, customarily hidden on the inside of a building, here becomes an impressive part of the exterior.*

Chinese children whose ancestors have lived here for generations chatter with equal facility in Chinese and English, and often use both languages in one sentence.

erable culture and education, who quickly established libraries, theatres, even a university. The first Jewish religious services were held in 1849, in Louis Franklin's tent on Jackson Street. (Though there was, in the early days, some resentment of the Chinese, racial and religious prejudice has never been fashionable in San Francisco.)

And thus, the beauty of the city is more than skin deep; more than a matter of hills and bay and cable cars, bridges, fog and sunshine. It is a beauty of spirit, and of diversity, and of the many peoples who have brought their own legacy, their own particular flavor, to the city.

Chinatown, North Beach, Fisherman's Wharf, Japantown, all add tremendously to the charm and fascination of the city. And there is the ever present gift of the Spanish who bequeathed to the city so many of its lingering, lovely names; California itself (from a mythical, gold-rich island in a fifteenth-century Spanish novel), Yerba Buena, Merced, Laguna Honda, Presidio, Embarcadero, El Camino Real.

The best known "neighborhood" is Chinatown, a magnet for San Franciscans and visitors alike, where some sixty-five thousand Chinese live and work.

The Chinese arrived in San Francisco (mostly from Canton) by the thousands in the 1850's, 60's, and 70's. Many took their hard-earned money and went back to China, but as many more stayed and settled into a tightly knit community of their own on Dupont Street (later Grant Avenue), clinging to their own customs, food and language. Even today, third and fourth generation Chinese children put in an after-hours stint at Chinese

A *polished window of the Bohemian Club turns a great glass eye on Taylor Street. The Club, founded by a group of newsmen in 1872, was once the refuge of the city's noted writers and artists. Today most of the now venerable club's members are businessmen.*

One girl and one pigeon stop for lunch by the fountain of Crown-Zellerbach Place; a motorized meter maid pauses for a chat; and a pretty girl turns heads on Broadway, where "topless" night clubs are now the prime attraction.

school to brush up on their ancestors' tongue and culture.

You can stroll the length of Chinatown's thoroughfare, Grant Avenue, in about an hour, from Bush Street, where it begins, to Broadway, where it ends in a whirl of traffic and neon. If you walk from south to north, it promises to get more interesting as you go along. At the downtown side of the avenue gaudy little shops offer merchandise from Hong Kong, Japan and Sioux City, prettily arranged to tempt the eye of the souvenir hunting visitor.

But as you press on toward California Street you discover the somber, elegant and expensive shops that carry Chinese antiques, furniture, and treasures of carved ivory and jade. And as you run the gantlet of tourist shops and night clubs you come to the "real" Chinatown that exists for the Chinese who live and work nearby.

Here is old St. Mary's Church, where services are conducted in English, Cantonese, and, most recently, Mandarin as well, for the thousands of newly-arrived Mandarin-speaking Chinese who are now settling in the city at the rate of some three thousand a year. Their specialized skills such as pastry-making, gold smithing, goldfish raising and flower arranging are flourishing in shops in the little by-streets of Chinatown.

Here are the grocery stores with Chinese vegetables, poultry shops with live chickens and ducks, fish shops with fish swimming endlessly round little tanks in the windows as they await their Kismet in the form of a little Chinese matron.

The modern interior of the First Methodist Church in Palo Alto sparkles as the bright California sunlight filters through its hundreds of small windows.

And though it may not be of any help to you, it is nice to know that there is a Chinese Telephone Answering Service.

Chinatown comes to an all-too-sudden end at Broadway, where one is jolted back into the Occidental world by a cacophony of traffic, "topless" night clubs, hot dog stands and pizza parlors.

A cheerful note on Broadway is the Bocce Ball, a San Francisco institution where a dedicated group of men play *bocce* in a back room, while out front one can drink capuccino and listen to Verdi and Puccini sung loudly and happily by both entertainers and customers.

North Beach, nestled in the valley between Russian and Telegraph Hills, is settled mostly by Italians from Veneto, Ticino and Sicily. The Italians brought with them their own food, music, and charm, and you can find them all in dozens of hospitable, small restaurants where you can dine cheaply, copiously and well.

The Sicilians became fishermen, as their ancestors had been, and created Fisherman's Wharf. The Wharf, a bit glossy now with gift shops and huge restaurants overlooking the water, is still a working wharf, where fishermen bring in some one hundred and twenty different kinds of fish, and crabs by the ton, and herein lies its charm. The wharf has been here a hundred years now, since the days when fishermen put out to sea in little boats with the yellow tinted sails of their native Sicily, and wrapped round their waists were great, wide satin scarfs instead of belts.

★

The complex approaches to the San Francisco-Oakland Bay Bridge are tolerated "south of Market," but the skyway that was to speed motorists along the Embarcadero to Marin County was stopped when it was only half built. It still obliterates the Ferry Building, however.

This gracious and well preserved house in Pacific Heights, left, was built in 1869 by lumber tycoon William Talbot as a wedding gift for his daughter. A 1911 "petit palais" on Nob Hill, center, is larger than it appears from its California Street entrance. In the back the lot drops off sharply, and the building stands a full five stories high.

A stately Georgian house in Pacific Heights, right, gives no evidence of passing time.

Until recently the small district spreading out from the intersection of Post and Buchanan Streets had no conspicuous landmark. Faded Victorian houses and small shops where many of the city's twelve thousand Japanese live gave no particular indication of their presence, other than an occasional tempura or sukiyaki sign.

The neighborhood, under the aegis of the San Francisco Redevelopment Agency, is now brushing up and presenting itself for the admiration of visitors. The Japanese Cultural and Trade Center, a new and dramatic string of handsome white buildings, which house the Japanese consulate, showrooms for Japanese industrial equipment, shops with Japanese gifts (everything from bonsai to pearls), a Japanese cabaret-restaurant, and a hotel with both Western and Japanese style rooms, will be the nucleus of a re-activated neighborhood. Dominated by a hundred-foot tall Peace Pagoda, Japantown is destined to become another fascinating San Francisco landmark.

★

It's hard to think of San Francisco without thinking of food. Good food in all its splendid diversity has been a tradition and a fetish ever since the forty-niners assembled in tents to eat egg roll; since the first Italian fisherman discovered that the bay was alive with crabs, and the first baker attempted to make French bread using the miner's sour dough as a starter.

The food of San Francisco is a composite of the city's own ethnic diversity and the profligate nature of California itself, with its abundant supplies of fresh

Don Quixote and Sancho Panza kneel to their creator, Cervantes, in Golden Gate Park. The father of Golden Gate Park, John McLaren, hated statues of any kind, and would have much preferred that they genuflect elsewhere.

101

San Franciscans love to dine out, and the city is full of intriguing restaurants to lure them. Always enthusiastic drinkers, San Franciscans invented the martini (named for the nearby town of Martinez) and the Tom and Jerry (after its inventor, bartender Jerry Thomas). Or so they say.

vegetables the year round, seafood, local and excellent cheese and wine.

Chinese, Japanese, Italian, French, Spanish, Mexican, Polynesian, Armenian, German, all have a special San Francisco flavor of their own. San Francisco has its own traditional and unique foods—crabs that steam in great cauldrons on the sidewalk at Fisherman's Wharf; sourdough bread with its thick, tangy crust; Joe's Special (a delicious confusion of ground beef, eggs, spinach, onions, and mushrooms that San Franciscans like to eat late at night at New Joe's); heavy, parmesan-dredged minestrone in mama-papa restaurants in North Beach; O-misu-taki in Japantown; shrimps stuffed to the size of chicken legs in tiny Filipino restaurants near Portsmouth Square.

And capuccinos. In Italy "capuccino" will get you coffee with a frothy head of milk on it, but in San Francisco "capuccino" is scalding hot chocolate laced with a big, marrow-warming dollop of brandy.

Perhaps no other city gazes at itself with such bemusement. Its citizens are constantly involved in comparisons. DO we have the finest symphony? ARE we a center of culture and art? ARE we the fairest city of them all? With much soul-seeking and searching, the inhabitants of San Francisco try to make it so.

Herb Caen, a San Francisco newspaper columnist who has been writing mash-notes to the city for a quarter of a century, recently wrote a tart reply to a criticism that

North Beach, nestled in the valley between Russian and Telegraph Hills, puzzles visitors who want to know where the beach is. Actually, the waters of the bay once nudged these streets, which have played equitable host to the Beat Generation of a decade ago and retains its fashionable bohemianism.

San Francisco's aquatic culture is reflected in the small craft, top left, which abound in the waters up and down the coast. The ferry to Sausalito, alas! is an antique, which citizens of the Bay Area hope however to resurrect, like the cable cars. For those who prefer dry land, Aquatic Park offers its own exotic pleasures.

the city was a trifle lacking in cultural achievements:

"If you define culture by the narrow terms of Rembrandts in the museums, symphony recordings, money for the ballet and facilities for the drama, we've never been in the running with the big boys, nor do I think we've ever claimed to be. It's just that weight for size, we've done extraordinarily well; it's the outlanders who come here expecting miracles.

"But a city's culture, as I see it, is an amalgam of taste, style, environment and heredity. It's something that exists in the roots and bones of a city, in its approach to day-to-day living, in its assessment of what's important and what isn't. Culture is what a city plays on its radio stations, what it prints in its newspapers... how people dress, the cars they drive, the food they eat, the drinks they drink. It's their houses, their furniture, their sense of humor, their élan, their attitude toward disaster and triumph.

"Culture is not what is displayed behind drawn curtains in dark rooms, but what is displayed for all to see: street signs, street clocks, street lamps, newsstands, and enough graceful old buildings to counterbalance the new hideosities.... Culture is Market Street, with its hot-dog smells, its crummy little movie houses, its young men with pants too tight, the blare of rock'n' roll, the daily parade of the lame, halt, blind and screaming. (Little old ladies are forever writing in to ask 'Why is Market Street so dirty?' Because it's a dirty street. Who says culture has to be neat?)"

Long an unsightly honky-tonk littered swath running

Beniamino Bufano's Penguins nestle in the plaza of the Golden Gateways Project, a huge new complex of business and residential structures near the Embarcadero.

(Overleaf).

San Francisco's architects and builders have always had a penchant for a kind of whimsical exaggeration of whatever style they chose to work in, as one can see in these various manifestations of Queen Anne. The house on the far right is painted in brilliant psychedelic colors. The lovely Tudor-Gothic house, lower center, which has a living room like the Great Hall of a feudal baron, was built by Bernard Maybeck in 1909.

katty-corner through the town, Market Street is about to be refurbished at a cost of twenty-four million dollars, as soon as the new cross-bay rapid transit system that now has it ripped up has finished its work of building subway stations. San Franciscans have been promised that for their money they will get "one of the most handsome and dramatic boulevards in the nation and in the world." Why not?

★

The prospect of change in the city causes violent spasms. Opponents of the new transit system tunneling under the bay to speed commuters from Oakland, Orinda, Berkeley and other surrounding "bedroom" communities claim that it will bring about the "Manhattanization" of San Francisco, the most damning epithet they can conceive.

Committees form overnight to proudly refuse government highways that promise to slash their way through the town. While other cities are eager for these Federal handouts with which to desecrate their habitations, thoughtful San Franciscans who still consider the city primarily a place to live, and only secondarily for the convenience of motor vehicles, shattered precedence a few years back by refusing a grant of several million dollars for a highway that would have destroyed their beautiful and beloved Embarcadero (the piers would henceforth have been visible only to motorists zipping by at sixty miles an hour). This was the first recorded

Despite its public image the University of California campus at Berkeley is usually serene and possessed of an almost bucolic charm.

112

A *city of many moods, styles and flavors, San Francisco still possesses independent entrepreneurs, a devoted coterie of bocce fans, and a restaurant for every purse and palate. Shoppers, right, browse along in front of I. Magnin's, whose tall windows reflect the palms of Union Square across the street.*

triumph of ordinary citizens over the ubiquitous concrete spreaders.

Similarly, conservationists have preserved the cable cars, a delight of immeasurable value, that in their clanging, charming way help bring millions of tourist dollars into the city coffers. The cable cars, once slated for doom by some penny-wise city official who thought odorous buses would be more economical, are now classified as national historical monuments and will permanently pursue their up-and-down course, unendangered by economists.

The same people (or others like them) fight fiercely (often unsuccesfully, but not always) against the construction of gigantic buildings that will dwarf the lovely hills and alter the character of the city.

The battle of "progress and expediency" versus conservation rages. Guardians of the city are alarmed by the fact that the bay is being filled with garbage at the rate of eight thousand tons a day, polluting the once fish-abundant waters, and producing the lucrative (for some) by-product of valuable flat land. The loss seems so gradual that few notice, but the statistics are dismaying.

One hundred years ago the bay covered seven hundred acres. Today it has dwindled to four hundred, and continues to decrease day by day, as the garbage-dumpers and land promoters gulp away at the remaining shallows.

Reminders of what once was give one a wistful twinge. In *The Western Gate* Joseph Henry Jackson

In the early 1900's wealthy San Franciscans began moving south to San Mateo County—"The Peninsula," where they built themselves imposing residences, taking European palaces as their inspiration. This formal French garden, a relic from the days of the great Peninsula establishments, is part of an estate in Hillsborough.

117

*S*an Franciscans like baseball, but fail to work up the passionate concern
Eastern fans do. However, San Francisco's Giants usually draw a full house.

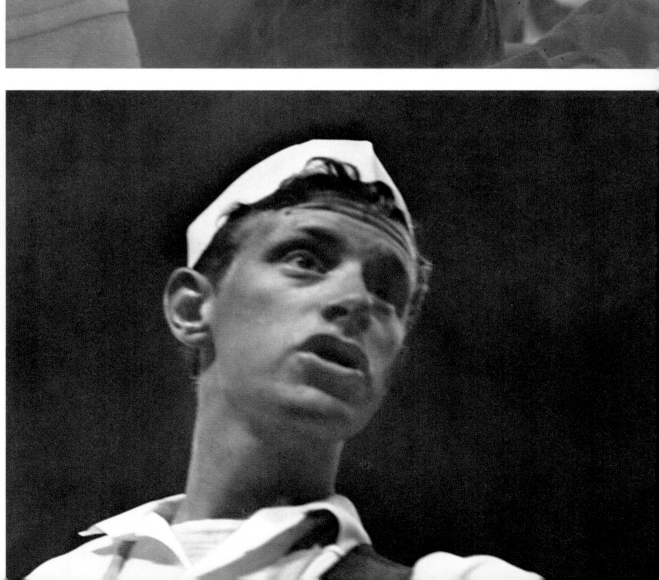

points out that in the early 1900's, the upper end of San Francisco Bay, where the San Joaquin and Sacramento Rivers merge with tidewaters, was famous for its oyster beds. And Frank Norris, in *McTeague*, an 1899 novel of San Francisco life, offhandedly describes "cheap restaurants, in whose windows one saw piles of unopened oysters weighed down by cubes of ice...."

But there are cheering notes among the gloom. The citizens of San Francisco, who began to be aware of what was happening a decade ago, have begun to defend the bay. There is now an Association of Bay Area Governments, a Bay-Delta Water Quality Control Program, Citizens for Regional and Recreational Parks, and a Bay Conservation and Development Commission.

A moratorium on filling is soon to be declared, and the direction of new development seems to be toward a rescue. Publicly owned bay-shore will be turned into parks, and more land will be purchased for that purpose.

An arm of Richardson's Bay was recently threatened with development, but conservationists rapidly raised a quarter of a million dollars, bought the land and turned it over to the Audubon Society as a wildfowl sanctuary.

Sea otters, the playful beasts with lovely coats that were once plentiful in San Francisco Bay until Russian fur hunters almost exterminated them, have recently been sighted again at Land's End. And native grey foxes, long since hunted into virtual extinction, have been reported there as well.

★

The Mission Dolores, San Francisco's oldest building, looks today very much as it did when it was completed by Indian neophytes in 1791. The little building in the Baroque ecclesiastical style of Mexico, with thick adobe brick walls and redwood roof trusses lashed together with rawhide strips, has withstood three major earthquakes.

A larger and more imposing basilica in the ornate Spanish Revivalist style was built next to the old Mission Dolores church in 1916, when one of the favorite Sunday diversions of San Franciscans was to make the considerable trip to the Mission. In the graveyard between the tow churches, from which this and the photograph on the preceding page were taken, lie the remains of many of the men who made California history. History was also made by financial tycoon and governor of the state Leland Stanford, who established Stanford University at Palo Alto in 1885, in memory of his son.

As concerned San Franciscans struggle, not to stop progress but to control it, to keep the city's unique character and not let it become another twentieth-century uni-city, they are, with a keen eye for cross-pollinating the best of the past with the needs of the present, developing their own special pattern of urban planning that other cities might be wise to emulate.

A classic example of San Francisco's ability to preserve the past and make a good commercial thing of it as well can be observed in the area known as Jackson Square.

Not a square at all, but a cluster of showrooms and offices covering five or six blocks from Montgomery and Sansome Streets to Pacific Avenue, the name comes from the Jackson Square Association which in 1951 took over acres of smoldering pre-earthquake warehouses and the long-shuttered boîtes of the Barbary Coast.

In most towns, "urban renewal" would have been slated. The bulldozers would have wrought their total destruction and unlovely modern "projects" would have replaced a bit of history with blank and faceless anonymity. Instead, the passion that San Franciscans feel for the history of their city triumphed. The area was rescued and converted into business premises for furniture, fabric and rug manufacturers, antique dealers and interior designers. Interior gutting, exterior paint, wit, love and imagination combined the old and charming buildings with the utility of modern design. Jackson Square is now a commercial success, a delight to walk through, and the good old buildings will live usefully for another century.

The white stone Spreckels House in Pacific Heights, in the style of a French Baroque palace, was built in 1912 for Adolph Spreckels, son of the sugar magnate Claus Spreckels. The Spreckels family later commissioned the architect, George Applegarth, to design the California Palace of the Legion of Honor.

*S*an Francisco in its blue mood—sun and fog and water, and the lovely Golden Gate Bridge rising, dreamlike, from the silent swirling water to the clouds.

Still another happy rescue was performed on Ghirardelli Square, a brand new San Francisco landmark, a howling commercial success that enchants San Franciscans and visitors alike, and the winner of an A.I.A. Award for excellence of design. Originally an old chocolate factory, the group of nineteenth-century buildings capped by a clock tower (said to be patterned after a Loire château) was turned into a fanciful complex of shops and restaurants set around a plaza with terraces, trees, flowers and fountains.

The tremendous commercial success of Ghirardelli Square inspired further conversions. Just a few blocks away, the Cannery (carved out of the brick skeleton of an abandoned Del Monte fruit cannery), is a fascinating compound of restaurants, shops, and a Farmer's Market.

A delightful orphan, rejected by the more practical-minded city of New York, has been adopted by San Francisco. An old open-topped double decker bus that used to transport New Yorkers joyfully up and down Fifth Avenue until it was banished by the exigencies of progress, now carries visitors from the Cannery to Ghirardelli Square to Fisherman's Wharf and back again. It's nice to know that somewhere in the world there's room for conveyances that combine pleasure with transportation.

And one more delightful anachronism may be about to return to San Francisco. The ferry boats, those gone-but-not-forgotten ghosts of the bay that used to steam so industriously back and forth with their loads of commuters, may make a triumphant comeback as the automobile multiplies itself into obsolescence.

The old ferries that connected San Francisco with Marin County until 1938 when the service was discontinued, made the run in forty-four minutes, while commuters drank their breakfast coffee and read their morning papers in peace and dignity.

Thirty years later, with such wonders as the bridge and the automobile to help him, a rush-hour motorist can expect one frustrating and boring hour at the wheel of his immobilized machine.

San Francisco's Mayor Alioto, a vigorous opponent of what he terms the "highway gang," conducted a study in cooperation with officials in Marin County to discover whether it would be economically feasible to again send ferries chugging back and forth across the bay. The answer, happily, was yes.

Right now, commuter boats that were formerly used for harbor sightseeing tours are busily transporting commuters between Tuburon, Belvedere and San Francisco, and the boat service will soon be expanded as soon as everyone decides from where to where.

All is not lost.

Joyce PETERSON.

IMPORTANT DATES IN SAN FRANCISCO'S HISTORY

1542

Juan Rodriguez Cabrillo is the first European to land in what is to become the state of California. He explores the coast of San Francisco but does not disembark there or see the bay.

1579

Sir Francis Drake sails up the coast, landing in what is now Drake's Bay and staying for about a month.

1595

Sebastian Rodriguez Cermenho sees and describes Monterey Bay.

1602

Sebastian Vizcaino visits and names Monterey Bay.

1769

Gaspar de Portola, leading a summer scouting party north from San Diego, reaches Monterey (*September* 30).

Sergeant José Francisco de Ortega of the Portola expedition is the first European to see San Francisco Bay (*November* 1)

1770

Portola and Fray Junipero Serra establish a Presidio and the Mission San Carlos Borromeo at Monterey.

1775

The *San Carlos*, piloted by Juan Manuel de Ayala, becomes the first ship to sail into the bay.

1776

Juan Bautista de Anza chooses the location for the Presidio and Mission of San Francisco (*March* 29).

Mission Dolores conducts its first mass (*June* 29). José Joaquin Moraga and Father Francisco Palóv with a group of settlers dedicate the Presidio on September 17. On October 9, they dedicate Mission Dolores.

1777

Father Serra, founder of the Upper California missions, visits the bay area; six missions soon follow in what is now metropolitan San Francisco.

1784

Father Serra dies at Carmel (*August* 28).

1796

The *Otter* of Boston, Ebenezer Dorr, Captain, becomes the first American ship to call at Monterey (*October* 29).

1806

Nikolai Petrovich Rezanof of the Russian American Company visits San Francisco in the ship *Juno*.

1810

Spanish-American Wars of Independence begin.

1812

Fort Ross is dedicated by the Russians.

1818

Hippolyte de Bouchard, an Argentine privateer, sacks Monterey (*November* 21).

1821

Mexican Independence declared (*February* 24).

1825

California becomes a province of Mexico.

1826

Jedediah Smith enters California after the first overland journey across the continent.

1828

Hudson Bay Company trappers enter California from the north.

1834

At a meeting in the Presidio, the Pueblo of Yerba Buena is formally established by the election of a town council (*December* 7).

1835

William A. Richardson is appointed port captain and pitches tent in Yerba Buena to become its first settler. The Calle de Fundacion, Foundation Street, the first street of the new town, is laid out. The new town is made a Mexican port of entry. After traders and whalers report its commercial possibilities, the U.S. tries to buy the bay from Mexico.

1841

Russia sells Fort Ross and leaves California.

First overland immigration; the Bidwell-Barleson wagon train reaches the San Joaquin Valley (*November* 4).

1846

U.S.-Mexican War. Yankee settlers led by Captain John Fremont seize Somona in the Bear Flag Rebellion and declare the California Republic (*June* 14). On July 7, Commodore John D. Sloat arrives in Monterey and takes possession for the U.S.

Two days later, Captain John B. Montgomery in the sloop of war *Portsmouth* enters San Francisco Bay and hoists the Stars and Stripes in the Plaza (now Portsmouth Plaza).

On July 13, war is officially declared between the U.S. and Mexico. *December* 6: General Stephen Kearney loses 21 dead at Battle of San Pascual to Californians under Andre Pico.

1847

Kearney and Commodore Robert F. Stockton defeat the Californians at the Battles of San Gabriel and La Mesa (*January* 8-9).

Pico surrenders to John Charles Fremont (*January* 13).

Yerba Buena's name is officially changed to San Francisco (*January* 30).

1848

January 24: James W. Marshall discovers gold on the America River near Colomba, California. The Gold Rush begins and will last until 1851.

The Treaty of Guadalupe Hidalgo ends the U.S.-Mexican War and transfers California to the U.S.

First Chinese arrive in *Gum Sahn* (Golden Hills). The Chinese population rises rapidly despite hostility and discrimination.

1849

The sidewheeler *California*, the first Gold Rush steamer, makes the first steam voyage around Cape Horn; arrives in San Francisco on February 28. Theatre and opera first appear. Fortune hunters descend on the city, giving it a distinctly boom town atmosphere.

State constitutional convention convenes at Monterey (*September* 1).

First state legislature meets at San Jose (*December* 15).

1850

September 9: California admitted to the Union.

1851

Vigilante Committee is formed to combat the widespread lawlessness resulting from the gold boom; hangs its first criminal, one John Jenkins, for stealing a safe.

First dry dock built.

1853

Telegraph introduced; links east and west coasts.

1854

Several weeks after his bankruptcy, Joshua Norton reappears on the streets of San Francisco proclaiming himself Norton I, Emperor of the U.S. and Mexico. For the next 26 years, he parades about the streets of the city dressed in an old army uniform, paying merchants with the special currency of his realm and becoming one of the first of the town's many colorful eccentrics.

Gas lighting introduced.

1856

Campaigning against crime, James King of William, editor of the *Evening Bulletin* is shot dead in the street by James Casey, a corrupt city supervisor. Second Vigilance Committee hangs Casey.

1860

First pony express arrives.

1864

Mark Twain arrives in San Francisco from Virginia City, Nevada; works as a journalist for the *Call* and the *Enterprise*.

1868

University of California chartered (*March* 23).

1869

First transcontinental railway completed (*May* 10).

1870

First oyster beds planted in the Bay.

1873

First cable car begins operating on Clay Street.

1876

Jack London, author of *Call of The Wild* and other great adventure novels, is born in the city.

Electric lighting and power is introduced.

1877

July 23: rioters burn and sack many Chinese laundries and businesses, indicating growing resentment of large numbers of Orientals.

Telephone is introduced.

1885

Union Iron Works produces first steel ship built on the Pacific Coast. First experimental farm is established in the San Francisco area by Luther Burbank.

1887

William Randolph Hearst acquires the *San Francisco Examiner* and quickly raises its circulation from 5,000 to 55,000 copies.

1891

Stanford University opens.

1906

April 18 : The Great Earthquake. Hundreds killed, $ 400 million damage done by the earthquake and resulting fire. The fire lasts for three days and destroys four-fifths of the city.

1915

Panama-Pacific International Exposition opens, planned to show the rebuilt city off to the world.

1916

Preparedness Day bombing; ten killed. Thomas Mooney and Warren K. Billings are indicted. The case becomes a *cause célèbre*, and many believe Mooney and Billings are railroaded.

1932

Present city charter goes into effect, providing elections for a Mayor, 11 city supervisors, and certain executive officials.

1934

July 5 : Two striking maritime workers are killed on " Bloody Thursday " and a four-day general strike results.

1936

The eight-mile-long San Francisco Bay Bridge opens.

1937

Golden Gate Bridge, with its 4200-foot suspension span across the Bay to Oakland, is completed at a cost of $ 35,000,000. For 27 years, it is the longest suspension bridge in the world (the record is beaten by the opening of New York's Verrazeano Bridge in 1964).

1939

The Golden Gate Exposition opens.

1945

United Nations Charter is drafted at international conference held in San Francisco.

1951

Peace Treaty with Japan ending the Second World War is signed in San Francisco.

1955-1960

Allen Ginsberg, Jack Kerouac, Lawrence Ferlinghetti, Gregory Corso and others make San Francisco a literary center and initiate the Beat Generation.

1958

New York Giants baseball team moves to San Francisco.

1962

Giants win the pennant.

1963

Alcatraz is closed as a Federal prison.

1964

Ghirardelli Square, a unique modern complex of shops, galleries, restaurants and theatres, opens in a nineteenth-century chocolate-spice-coffee-woolen works overlooking Aquatic Park. Berkeley student rebellion initiates a period of nation-wide student protests and demonstrations. First phase of Golden Gateway Center waterfront renewal project completed.

1967

Restoration completed of the monumental 50-year-old Greco-Romanesque rotunda housing the Palace of Fine Arts. The American Conservatory Theatre becomes part of San Francisco's cultural scene. Haight-Ashbury becomes center for hippies, and generates the new attitudes of America's youth culture. Several new skyscrapers rise on the San Francisco skyline.

1968

Japanese Cultural and Trade Center, a three block Japanese showcase and shopping area is dedicated. A 120,000-square-foot addition to Ghirardelli Square is opened in April. Opening of ABC Marine World in Redwood City, largest marine recreation and educational complex in the west.

1969-70

The Cannery, a $ 9.5 million complex of shops, restaurants, markets and galleries opens on the site of the old Del Monte Fruit Cannery near Fisherman's Wharf. A $ 75,000 decorative gateway is created to frame the entrance to Chinatown. Earthquake tremors along the San Andreas Fault.

The hippie movement subsides into San Francisco history.

SAN FRANCISCO BAY AREA

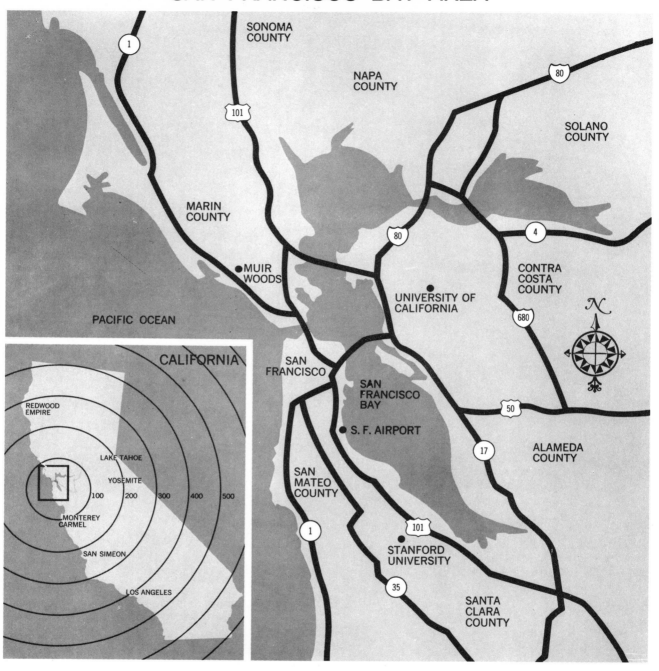

DOWNTOWN SAN FRANCISCO

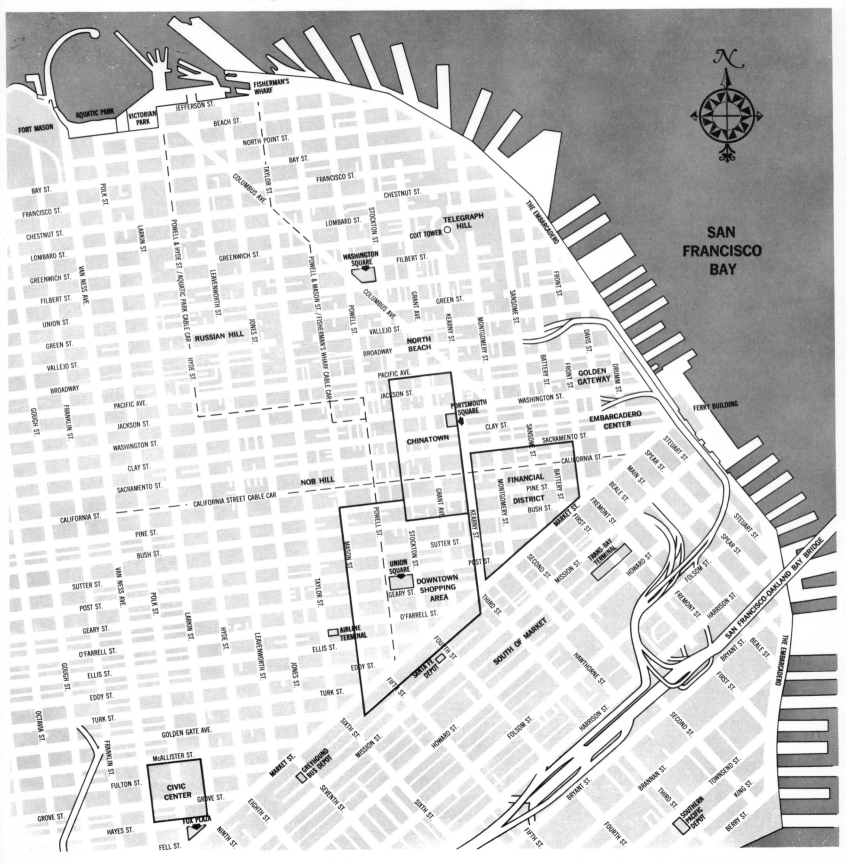

FORT MASON

AQUATIC PARK

VICTORIAN PARK

FISHERMAN'S WHARF

JEFFERSON ST.

BEACH ST.

NORTH POINT ST.

BAY ST.

FRANCISCO ST.

CHESTNUT ST.

TELEGRAPH HILL

COIT TOWER

WASHINGTON SQUARE

FILBERT ST.

BAY ST.

FRANCISCO ST.

CHESTNUT ST.

LOMBARD ST.

GREENWICH ST.

FILBERT ST.

UNION ST.

GREEN ST.

VALLEJO ST.

BROADWAY

POLK ST.

VAN NESS AVE.

LARKIN ST.

POWELL & HYDE ST./AQUATIC PARK CABLE CAR

LEAVENWORTH ST.

HYDE ST.

JONES ST.

RUSSIAN HILL

POWELL ST.

COLUMBUS AVE.

POWELL & MASON ST./FISHERMAN'S WHARF CABLE CAR

STOCKTON ST.

TAYLOR ST.

LOMBARD ST.

GREENWICH ST.

COLUMBUS AVE.

VALLEJO ST.

BROADWAY

GRANT AVE.

GREEN ST.

KEARNY ST.

MONTGOMERY ST.

SANSOME ST.

FRONT ST.

BATTERY ST.

FRONT ST.

DAVIS ST.

DRUMM ST.

SAN FRANCISCO BAY

THE EMBARCADERO

GOLDEN GATEWAY

FERRY BUILDING

NORTH BEACH

PACIFIC AVE.

JACKSON ST.

CHINATOWN

PORTSMOUTH SQUARE

CLAY ST.

WASHINGTON ST.

SACRAMENTO ST.

CALIFORNIA ST.

EMBARCADERO CENTER

GOUGH ST.

FRANKLIN ST.

PACIFIC AVE.

JACKSON ST.

WASHINGTON ST.

CLAY ST.

SACRAMENTO ST.

CALIFORNIA STREET CABLE CAR

NOB HILL

GRANT AVE.

FINANCIAL DISTRICT

PINE ST.

MONTGOMERY ST.

BUSH ST.

BATTERY ST.

MARKET ST.

FIRST ST.

FREMONT ST.

BEALE ST.

MAIN ST.

SPEAR ST.

STEUART ST.

CALIFORNIA ST.

PINE ST.

BUSH ST.

MASON ST.

POWELL ST.

STOCKTON ST.

SUTTER ST.

POST ST.

KEARNY ST.

UNION SQUARE

DOWNTOWN SHOPPING AREA

GEARY ST.

O'FARRELL ST.

THIRD ST.

SECOND ST.

MISSION ST.

TRANS-BAY TERMINAL

HOWARD ST.

FREMONT ST.

HARRISON ST.

SPEAR ST.

STEUART ST.

SAN FRANCISCO-OAKLAND BAY BRIDGE

THE EMBARCADERO

VAN NESS AVE.

POLK ST.

LARKIN ST.

HYDE ST.

LEAVENWORTH ST.

JONES ST.

TAYLOR ST.

SUTTER ST.

POST ST.

GEARY ST.

O'FARRELL ST.

ELLIS ST.

AIRLINE TERMINAL

EDDY ST.

TURK ST.

POWELL ST.

FIFTH ST.

SANTA FE DEPOT

FOURTH ST.

SOUTH OF MARKET

HAWTHORNE ST.

FOLSOM ST.

BRYANT ST.

HARRISON ST.

FIRST ST.

BEALE ST.

SECOND ST.

OCTAVIA ST.

GOUGH ST.

FRANKLIN ST.

TURK ST.

GOLDEN GATE AVE.

McALLISTER ST.

CIVIC CENTER

FULTON ST.

GROVE ST.

GROVE ST.

FOX PLAZA

HAYES ST.

FELL ST.

MARKET ST.

NINTH ST.

EIGHTH ST.

GREYHOUND BUS DEPOT

MISSION ST.

SEVENTH ST.

SIXTH ST.

HOWARD ST.

SIXTH ST.

FIFTH ST.

BRYANT ST.

FOLSOM ST.

BRANNAN ST.

SOUTHERN PACIFIC DEPOT

THIRD ST.

FOURTH ST.

TOWNSEND ST.

KING ST.

BERRY ST.

SECOND ST.

LIST OF ILLUSTRATIONS

PRINTED IN FRANCE THE 30 TH OF JULY 1970
FOR TUDOR PUBLISHING COMPANY, NEW YORK.
THE BLACK AND WHITE ILLUSTRATIONS WERE
PRINTED BY BRAUN IN MULHOUSE AND THE
ILLUSTRATIONS IN COLOR BY IMPRIMERIE
MODERNE DU LION IN PARIS

All the photographs are by Peter Fink with the exception of the following pages
Charles Lénars, Back Cover IV, p. 42 California Street.